# COUNTRY TOPICS
## FOR CRAFT PROJECTS

# MEXICO

**ANITA GANERI**
**and**
**RACHEL WRIGHT**

Illustrated by John Shackell

FRANKLIN WATTS
NEW YORK • CHICAGO • LONDON • TORONTO • SYDNEY

This symbol appears on some pages throughout this book. It indicates that adult supervision is advisable for that activity.

**Library of Congress Cataloging-in-Publication Data**

Ganeri, Anita, 1961-
Mexico / by Anita Ganeri and Rachel Wright.
   p.  cm. -- (Country topics for craft projects)
Includes index.
ISBN 0-531-14316-3
1.  Handicraft--Mexico--Juvenile literature.  2.  Mexico--Social life
and customs--Juvenile literature.  [1.  Mexico.]  I.  Wright,
Rachel.  II Title.  III.  Series.
TT28.G36  1994
745.5--dc20                     94-7099
                             CIP
Paperback edition published in 1995     AC
ISBN 0-531-15278-2

© Franklin Watts 1994

Franklin Watts
A Division of Grolier Publishing
Sherman Turnpike
Danbury, CT 06816

10 9 8 7 6 5 4 3 2 1

**Editor:** Hazel Poole
**Designer:** Sally Boothroyd
**Photography:** Peter Millard
**Artwork:** John Shackell
**Picture Research:** Juliet Duff

Printed in the United Kingdom

# CONTENTS

# Introducing Mexico

*¡Buenos días! y Bienvenido!*
Hello, and a very warm
welcome to Mexico! Before
you set off on your travels,
here are some fascinating and
useful facts about the country.

## MEXICO IN THE WORLD

Mexico is a long, thin country in the southernmost part of North America. It covers an area of 760,000 square miles (1,958,200 sq km) and has a population of about 90 million. Its capital is Mexico City, one of the largest and most crowded cities in the world. Other major cities include Guadalajara, Netzahualcóyotl, and Monterrey. From the map you can see that Mexico has long coastlines. The Pacific Ocean lies to the west and southwest. The Gulf of Mexico and the Caribbean Sea (parts of the Atlantic Ocean) lie to the east. On land, Mexico has borders with the United States on the north and with Guatemala and Belize on the southeast.

## THE MEXICAN FLAG

The Mexican flag has three vertical stripes in green, white, and red. Each color has a special meaning. Green is for independence, white is for religion, and red stands for unity. In the center of the flag is Mexico's coat of arms. It shows an eagle perched on a prickly pear cactus, holding a snake in its beak. According to legend, the Aztecs (see page 24) built their capital, Tenochtitlán, on the spot where they saw the eagle eating the snake. Mexico City now stands on the sight of Tenochtitlán. The flag was adopted in 1821, when Mexico gained its independence from Spain.

## GOVERNMENT

Mexico's official name is *los Estados Unidos Mexicanos* – the United Mexican States. The country is a republic, divided into 31 states and one federal district. It has a democratic form of government. The president is the head of state and is elected for six years at a time. Parliament is made up of a General Congress, which is divided into the Senate and the Chamber of Deputies.

## MEXICAN MONEY

The Mexican currency is called the *peso*, written as MX$. One *peso* is divided into 100 *centavos*. To prevent confusion with American dollars, prices are sometimes written as, for example, $25mn. The "mn" stands for *moneda nacional* (national money).

## MEXICAN LANGUAGES

The words in the "Say it in" boxes throughout this book are in Spanish, the official language of Mexico. Mexican Spanish is almost identical to the Spanish spoken in Spain, except that it has Indian words mixed in with it. These come from the Náhuatl language. Other Indian languages still spoken in Mexico include Mixtec, Maya, and Zapotec. These date from the days before the Spanish conquest of Mexico in the sixteenth century. Almost everyone in Mexico speaks and understands Spanish, though.

**Say it in Spanish**
*¡ Buenos días!*– hello, good morning
*dinero* – money
*banco* – bank
*timbre* – stamp
*correo* – post office
*español* – Spanish
*mapa* – map

Mexico is a fascinating country with ancient ruins, modern cities, deserts, jungles, and beautiful beaches. With such a variety of sights to see and places to explore, it's not surprising that six million tourists visit Mexico each year.

## BAJA CALIFORNIA

Baja California is a long, spindly finger of land sticking out into the Pacific Ocean. About halfway down the peninsula lies the town of Guerrero Negro. It is famous for its lagoon, called Scammon's Lagoon. Each year, thousands of gray whales migrate there from the Bering Sea in the Arctic, to breed.

## MEXICAN GEOGRAPHY

On the map of Mexico below you can see the different geographical regions, the main mountains, rivers, and so on. There are also suggestions for places to visit. Mexico has a wide range of landscapes within its borders. Two thirds of the country is covered with high mountains and hills, including the western and eastern Sierra Madre. The highest mountain is Citlaltépetl at 18,700 feet (5,700 m). It is one of a chain of volcanic mountains running across the southern part of the country. The main rivers are the Río Grande and the Balsas. The Mexican climate varies from place to place. The north is mostly hot, dry desert. The south is tropical. The tops of the highest mountains are always covered with snow.

## MEXICO CITY

Mexico City is a mixture of ancient Aztec temples and palaces, grand Spanish churches and cathedrals, and modern high-rise apartment buildings as well as poor sections and slums. A huge square, called the Zócalo, lies at the heart of the city. This was also the site of the main square of the Aztec city of Tenochtitlán (see page 24), where the Great Temple and royal palace stood.

## THE COPPER CANYON

The Copper Canyon, or Barranca del Cobre, lies in the western Sierra Madre mountains. For the most dramatic view of the canyon, take the train. The journey lasts for about 12 hours, passing through 86 tunnels and over 39 bridges! But it's worth it. The gorges that make up the Copper Canyon are up to 4,000 feet (1,200 m) deep and 5,000 (1,500 m) wide, and are carved out of the mountainsides by the Urique River.

## ACAPULCO

The city of Acapulco on the southwest coast is Mexico's most famous resort. It has beaches, hotels, and restaurants galore. But one of its most amazing attractions are the cliff divers of La Quebrada. They dive off the sheer cliffs, from heights of up to 150 feet (45 m), into a narrow inlet of sea below. The water is only 12 feet (3.5 m) deep there.

## DESERT LIFE

The deserts of north and north-western Mexico are home to some amazing plants and animals. Among them are giant saguaro cacti, which can grow over 40 feet (12 m) tall, and prickly pear cacti. There are also coyotes, rattlesnakes, prairie dogs, and gila monsters, one of only two types of poisonous lizards.

## CHICHÉN ITZÁ

The ruins of the ancient Mayan city of Chichén Itzá are found on the Yucatán Peninsula in the southeast of Mexico. The city was at its greatest between the sixth and tenth centuries A.D. One of the best preserved buildings is a pyramid, El Castillo (The Castle). The temple at the top was reached by a flight of 365 steps, one for each day of the year.

**Say it in Spanish**
*montaña* – mountain
*volcán* – volcano
*río* – river
*ciudad* – city
*desierto* – desert
*cacto* – cactus
*culebra* – snake

7

# Food and Drink

In Mexico, people eat three meals a day – *desayuno* (breakfast), *comida* (a large lunch), and *cena* (a light supper). The staple foods in the Mexican diet are *tortillas* (flat corn cakes), *frijoles* (beans), and *chiles* (chili peppers). Many Mexicans grow their own food or buy it fresh from the local markets.

## TASTY TORTILLAS

Maize (corn) is the most important crop grown in Mexico and the most important source of food. It is ground into meal (like flour) and made into thin, round cakes called *tortillas.* These can be eaten plain or filled with chicken, meat, cheese, or beans. They are called *tacos* when they are filled, folded, then fried. They are called *enchiladas* when they are filled, rolled up, and covered in spicy sauce. And they are called *tostadas* when they are fried and served flat with a topping. Don't worry – you'll soon get the hang of it! *Tortillas* are often stuffed with *frijoles* (beans), or used to scoop up helpings of beans. Many Mexicans eat beans every day, seasoned with hot chili peppers. You can find out how to make another Mexican speciality, *guacamole,* on pages 10 – 11.

## CHOCOLATE MONEY

Chocolate is made from the beans of the cacao tree, which originally grew wild in Mexico. The Aztecs valued chocolate so much that they used cocoa beans as currency. They also drank chocolate spiced with peppers. Modern-day Mexicans prefer their chocolate flavored with sugar and vanilla. A popular dish for special occasions is turkey with *mole,* a sauce made of chocolate, chili peppers, and sesame seeds.

## WHAT TO DRINK?

If you are hot and thirsty, try a refreshing glass of an *agua fresca*. This is fruit juice mixed with sugar and water. There are many different varieties.

Mexico is famous for its very strong alcoholic drinks, which are made from cacti and other desert plants. Tequila is made from the sap of the spiky maguey plant. The sap is pressed out, mixed with sugar, fermented, distilled, and bottled. As a final touch, a worm is added to each bottle! Tequila is traditionally drunk with salt and lime. When the bottle is empty, the worm has to be eaten!

Shopping List

huevos - eggs
pan - bread
mantequilla - butter
carne - meat
pavo - turkey
gazpacho - chilled, spicy
vegetable soup
aguacate - avocado pear
elote - corn on the cob
queso - cheese
agua - water
tuña - fruit of the prickly pear cactus

# Mexican Dip

The next time you throw a party, why not give it a real Mexican flavor by serving a bowl of guacamole, surrounded by tortilla chips for dipping?

**To make guacamole . . .**

**YOU WILL NEED:**

MIXING BOWL

SERVING BOWL

2 MEDIUM-SIZED RIPE AVOCADOS

½ MEDIUM-SIZED ONION

½ CLOVE OF GARLIC

3 TABLESPOONS OF READY-MADE TACO SAUCE

PINCH OF SALT

¼ OF A LIME

BAG OF TORTILLA CHIPS

GARLIC PRESS

SHARP KNIFE

FORK

SPOON

CUTTING BOARD

**Spice advice**

If you don't like very hot and spicy foods, use mild taco sauce for this recipe. If, however, you want to make your taste buds really tingle, buy hot taco sauce instead.

**1.** Peel the onion. Chop it up as finely as you can and put it in the mixing bowl. If you have a food processor, ask an adult to show you how to use it to chop up the onion.

**2.** Crush the ½ clove of garlic into the bowl and add the taco sauce.

**3.** Squeeze the juice of the lime into the mixing bowl and stir well.

**4.** Cut the avocados in half and dig out the pits with a spoon. Put the pits to one side.

**5.** Scoop the flesh of the avocados into the bowl with a spoon. Make sure you scrape the skins well.

**6.** Chop the avocado flesh with the knife and fork.

**7.** Using the fork, mash the avocado flesh until it is almost smooth. Add a pinch of salt and stir.

**8.** Spoon the guacamole into the serving dish. Surround the dish with tortilla chips and potato chips, or if you prefer, scrubbed raw vegetables cut into sticks, and let your guests help themselves.

### Dip Tip
Don't make your guacamole too far in advance, otherwise the avocado will darken. To slow down this darkening process, try leaving the avocado pits in the guacamole until you are ready to eat it.

# Life in Mexico

## PEOPLE AND THEIR ORIGINS

About 90 million people live in Mexico and the population is getting bigger all the time. Some three-quarters of the people live in towns and cities. Only about one quarter live in the countryside. Many people are very poor. Some try to make their way, illegally, across the border into the U.S. to look for work. Most are caught and sent back again.

Most Mexicans are descended from Spanish and Indian ancestors. They are called *mestizos*. There are also about 5 million Indians who have kept their traditional customs, culture, and languages. The biggest group are the Nahua, whose ancestors were the Aztecs.

## TRADE AND INDUSTRY

In the last 30 years, Mexico has made great efforts to strengthen its economy and modernize its industries. It manufactures and exports iron, steel, and motor vehicles. It also exports sugar and coffee. It is a leading producer of oil (from the Gulf of Mexico) and silver. Tourism is one of Mexico's most important industries, providing valuable foreign income and jobs.

## On the Farm

Approximately one quarter of all Mexicans live in small villages or on farms. The main crops are maize, coffee, bananas, wheat, and potatoes. Avocados, chili peppers, lemons, tomatoes, and vanilla are also grown. Cattle are raised for beef and milk. Farmers take their produce to market to sell or trade for other goods. Many farms are very small and very poor. There are also *ejidos*, community farms worked by groups of farmers, and large *haciendas*, country estates owned by rich landowners.

## Going to School

All Mexican schools used to be under the control of the Roman Catholic Church. Today the government is in charge of education. By law, children have to go to school from the age of six to 14. In the countryside, however, many children leave school early to help their parents in the fields. The oldest university in Mexico is the National Autonomous University of Mexico, in Mexico City. It was founded in 1551.

## What People Wear

In the towns and cities, most Mexicans wear clothes similar to those worn in the United States. In the villages people wear more traditional clothes. They wear wide-brimmed sombreros to protect them from the hot sun. Ponchos or serapes (shawls) are worn in cold weather. You can find out how to make your own poncho on pages 15–17. Clothes are handwoven and embroidered in bright colors. Each region has its own distinctive set of colors and designs.

**Say it in Spanish**
*fábrica* – factory
*granja* – farm
*pueblo* – village
*escuela* – school
*mercado* – market
*plata* – silver
*café* – coffee
*azúcar* – sugar

# Arts and Crafts

If you visit a market in Mexico, you'll find a wide range of locally made handicrafts. You'll be able to buy handwoven baskets and embroidered cloth, pottery, carpets, and silverware. Market prices are not usually fixed, so be ready to haggle!

## CARPETS

Carpets are woven in brightly colored yarns on large looms. Their designs include ancient symbols such as the sun and moon, which represent the forces of nature, and animals and birds which represent life. A medium-sized carpet takes four people about 30 days to make and uses at least 140,000 knots.

## MODERN ART

One of modern Mexico's most famous artists was Diego Rivera (1886–1957). He painted bold, colorful murals of scenes from Mexican life, many of which illustrated historical events, such as the Mexican Revolution, and social problems as their themes.

A Diego Rivera mural of an Aztec market.

### BEAUTIFUL POTS

Mexico is famous for its decorative pottery. Pots are often brightly painted with scenes from ancient myths and legends as well as everyday people and places.

# Patterned Ponchos

Mexican ponchos or *jorongos* are often striped and colorful.

**YOU WILL NEED:**

THREAD

WOOL OR ACRYLIC YARN

PEN

SCISSORS

NEEDLES

PINS

RULER

CARDBOARD

DIFFERENT COLORED FELT

A PIECE OF LIGHTWEIGHT WOOLEN MATERIAL WIDE ENOUGH TO REACH ACROSS YOUR BODY FROM JUST BEYOND ONE OUTSTRETCHED ELBOW TO THE OTHER. THE MATERIAL MUST ALSO BE LONG ENOUGH TO REACH FROM YOUR KNEES OVER YOUR SHOULDER TO THE BACK OF YOUR KNEES.

The edges of the poncho on page 17 are covered with a blanket stitch. To sew a row of blanket stitches . . .

**1.** Push a threaded needle through some material from back to front. Then, working from left to right, push the needle through to the back of the material and bring it out between the material and thread.

**2.** Pull the thread through the loop. Start again at step 1.

**3.** Try to keep your stitches the same length and the same distance apart.

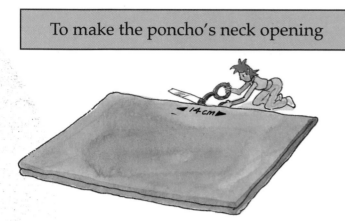

**4.** Fold the woolen fabric in half, as shown, and cut a slit about 7 in (17 cm) long on the center of the fold.

**5.** Using the slit as a baseline, draw a triangle about 4 in (10 cm) long. Cut out the triangle, slip the poncho over your head, and check that the neck opening is the right size.

**6.** Turn in the raw edges along the neck opening and pin them down. Thread a needle with a length of yarn and, using the blanket stitch, sew a narrow hem along the neckline. Remove the pins.

## Make the edges neat

**7.** Turn in the raw edges along the bottom and sides of the poncho and pin them down. Sew the edges down with a blanket stitch and remove the pins.

## To make a tassel

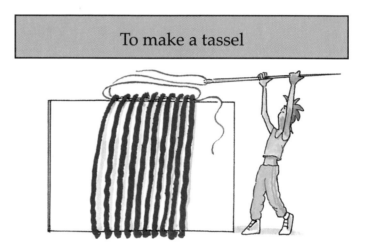

**8.** Decide how long you want your tassels to be and cut a piece of cardboard to the same length. Wind some yarn around the length of the cardboard. Thread a needle and pass it under the top of the tassel a couple of times. Tie the thread in a knot.

**9.** Cut the tassel through at the bottom. Wind the thread around the tassel, near the top. Pull it through the top of the tassel and tie it in a knot to finish. Make more tassels and sew them onto the bottom of your poncho.

## To decorate the poncho

**10.** Find some simple Mexican designs that you like and copy them onto the pieces of felt. Cut out these designs and pin them onto your poncho. Sew them into place and remove the pins.

**11.** Before you wear your poncho for the first time, iron all its blanket-stitched hems.

Ponchos are also worn in other countries such as Peru and Bolivia.

# Sports and Leisure

Sports have been an important part of Mexican life for hundreds of years. Like everything else in the country, popular sports are a mixture of ancient and modern traditions with Indian, Spanish, and American influences.

## SOCCER CRAZY

Mexicans are mad about soccer. Although it has never won the World Cup, Mexico has hosted it twice, in 1970 and 1986. On each occasion, the final was played in the 100,000-seat Azteca Stadium in Mexico City. The top national clubs are América (of Mexico City) and Guadalajara. Soccer is also shown on television.

## BASKETBALL OLD AND NEW

Basketball is a very popular sport in modern Mexico. It was a favorite of the Maya, too. They played their own version of the game, called *ollamalitzli*. Players had to get a solid rubber ball through a small stone ring set in the wall of the ball court. They were only allowed to touch the very hard ball with their knees, hips, and elbows. This caused a lot of injuries.

## OLYMPIC CITY

The 1968 Olympic Games were held in Mexico City. The main stadium was the Estadio Olimpico Mexico 68 which holds 80,000 spectators and is designed to look like the cone of a volcano. There is a mosaic by Diego Rivera (see page 14) over the main entrance.

## BULLFIGHTING

Because of Spanish influence on Mexico, bullfighting has become the country's national sport. There are two bullrings in Mexico City, including the largest in the world which seats about 55,000 people. The bravest matadors (bullfighters) become great heroes. Sunday is bullfighting day in the capital.

## JAI ALAI

Jai alai is a game similar to squash; it is based on the Spanish game, pelota and played on a long court. The players have curved, basketlike rackets attached to their arms. They use these to hit the ball very hard against the walls. Jai alai is a fast, furious, and very exciting game to watch.

**Say it in Spanish**
*toro* – bull
*futbol* – soccer
*balón* – soccer ball
*pelota* – ball (e.g. tennis ball)
*deporte* – sport
*equipo* – team
*televisión* – television

# Festival Time!

There are holidays, festivals, and fiestas throughout the year in Mexico. Many of them have religious themes. About 90 percent of Mexicans are Roman Catholics. Some Indians still follow their ancient religions which are based around the worship of the spirits of nature. There are also festivals to celebrate good harvests. (You can find out more about the festival of the Day of the Dead on page 22).

## INDEPENDENCE DAYS

Mexico's independence days are celebrated on the 15th and 16th of September annually. Mexico gained its independence from Spain in 1821. The biggest fiesta takes place in Mexico City. The president recites a special hymn of freedom in the Zócalo, then the celebrations begin with fireworks, folk dancing, music, and horse races.

## GUADALUPE DAY

The most important religious festival is Guadalupe Day, celebrated on December 12. It is the feast day of the patron saint of Mexico, Our Lady of Guadalupe. According to legend, this was the day in 1531 on which the saint appeared to a local Indian girl on Tepeyac Hill in Mexico City.

Fiesta time in Mexico.

Independence celebrations in the Zócalo.

Mexican boy trying to break open the piñata.

## MEXICAN HAT DANCE

**M**usic and dancing are vital parts of any fiesta. One of the most popular folk dances is the Mexican hat dance, the *jarabe tapatío*. The women dancers wear a costume called a *china poblana*, made up of a red and green beaded skirt, an embroidered short-sleeved blouse, and a colorful sash. The story goes that this costume is named after a Chinese princess who was sold as a slave in Mexico. She dedicated her life to helping the poor and wore this costume as she worked.

## MUSIC TO THE EARS

**M**exico is famous for its bands of strolling musicians, called *mariachis*. They sing and play guitars, violins, and trumpets. There are also marimba bands who play instruments resembling large, wooden xylophones. Some Indian groups still play the ancient music of their ancestors, on traditional instruments such as gourd rattles, wooden flutes, and seashells.

## CHRISTMAS CHEER

**O**n the nine days before Christmas Day, children all over Mexico act out Mary and Joseph's journey to Bethlehem. These special parades are called *posadas*. After each night's posada, the children break open papier-mâché animals, called *piñatas*. These are full of candy, toys, and fruit. On Twelfth Night (January 6), parents also fill their children's shoes with gifts.

**Say it in Spanish**
*fiesta* – festival
*música* – music
*baile* – dance
*juguete* – toy
*Día de Navidad* – Christmas Day
*regalo* – present, gift

# Day of the Dead

The Day of the Dead, which is celebrated on November 1 and 2, is Mexico's most fantastic festival. It marks the time when the souls of the dead come back to Earth for just a few brief hours.

During the festival, tables are set up in the family home and decorated with flowers, fruit, candles, and pictures of the saints. At the appropriate time, they are also covered with a feast of food and drink. Attracted by the scent of the flowers and incense, the souls of the dead return to their families, usually unseen and unheard, to take up the essence of the food. After that, they go back to their resting place and the living family share the feast with their friends.

Many Mexicans also take flowers and candles to the graves of their loved ones during the festival, as well as more food and drink.

During the Day of the Dead festival, children buy sugar skulls bearing the names of their friends, to give as presents.

## SUGAR SKULLS

**1.** Roll the marzipan into a ball and then shape it into a skull. (If the marzipan sticks to the palms of your hands, sprinkle it with a little powdered sugar.)

**2.** Press two eye sockets into the skull with the end of a wooden spoon and put a cake decoration in each hole. Carve teeth and other features with a toothpick.

**3.** Decorate the skull with icing, colored foil, or anything else you like, and write or stick your name on it.

A LITTLE POWDERED SUGAR

A TUBE OF COLORED ICING

**YOU WILL NEED:**

AND DECORATING NOZZLES

SMALL CAKE DECORATIONS (DRAGÉES)

TOOTHPICK

WOODEN SPOON

9oz (250g) READY-MADE WHITE MARZIPAN

Mexico's history is long and fascinating. It can be split into two periods, before and after the arrival of the Spanish *conquistadors* (conquerors) in 1521. Before this date, a series of Indian civilizations grew up in Mexico. They were highly advanced, with great cities, counting systems, and calendars. You can find out about some of them below. There is more about the history of Mexico after the Spanish conquest on page 28.

## THE OLMECS

The first great Mexican civilization was that of the Olmecs from 1200 to 400 B.C. Their name means "people from the land of rubber." The Olmecs are famous for the huge stone heads they carved out of basalt. Some of the heads are 10 feet (3 meters) tall and weigh over 20 tons. They probably show ruler-priests of the Olmecs.

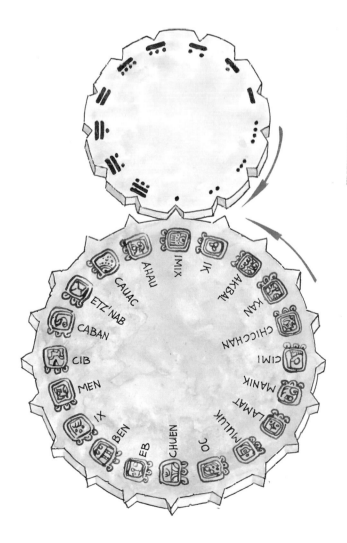

## THE MAYA

The Maya civilization of southern Mexico lasted from 500 B.C. to A.D. 1450. Its greatest cities were built at Chichén Itzá (see page 7) and Tikal. The Mayans were skilled astronomers and mathematicians. They devised an accurate 365-day solar calendar, made up of 18 months of 20 days each and five spare days. They had a separate calendar for religious events. The Maya also had a complicated system of picture writing, with some 500 symbols.

## The Toltecs

The warlike Toltecs flourished from A.D. 900 to 1200. Their capital was the city of Tula. The main god of the Toltecs, and of many other Indian groups, was the plumed serpent, Quetzalcoatl. He was the god of nature, air, and earth, symbolized by a serpent with quetzal bird feathers. Emperors and people of high rank were also permitted to wear quetzal feather headdresses as status symbols. Quetzals still live in the jungles of Central America but are very rare.

The sacred quetzal bird.

## The Aztec Empire

The Aztecs were at their height of power from A.D. 1300 to 1521. Originally a wandering tribe, they established a huge, well-organized capital city on the site of modern Mexico City. Tenochtitlán was built on an island in Lake Texcoco (later drained by the Spanish). Three great causeways linked it to the mainland. In its heyday, the city was home to 100,000 people.

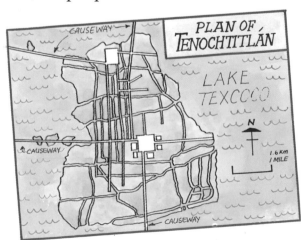

PLAN OF TENOCHTITLÁN
CAUSEWAY
LAKE TEXCOCO
N
1.6 Km / MILE
CAUSEWAY
CAUSEWAY

## Sacrifices to the Sun

The Aztecs believed that human sacrifice was needed to make sure the sun rose every day. The victims were killed and their hearts and blood offered to the sun god. Most of the victims were prisoners of war.

# Mosaic Masks

Aztec craftsmen made beautiful mosaic masks which may have been worn by priests during religious ceremonies. This mask of the god Quetzalcoatl is decorated with small pieces of turquoise.

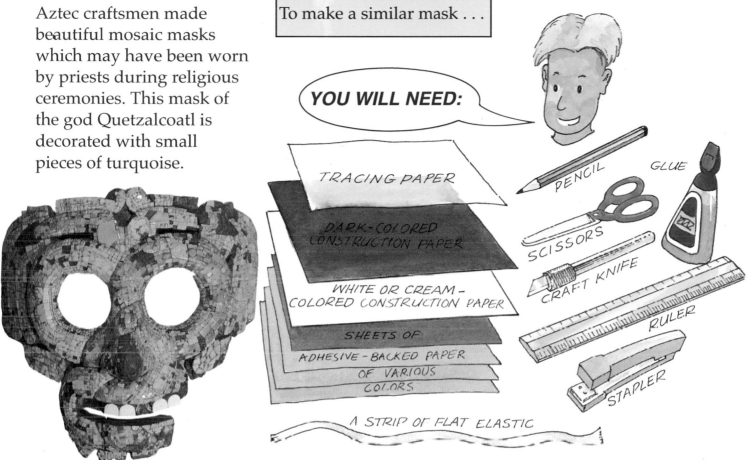

To make a similar mask . . .

**YOU WILL NEED:**

TRACING PAPER

DARK-COLORED CONSTRUCTION PAPER

WHITE OR CREAM-COLORED CONSTRUCTION PAPER

SHEETS OF ADHESIVE-BACKED PAPER OF VARIOUS COLORS

A STRIP OF FLAT ELASTIC

PENCIL

GLUE

SCISSORS

CRAFT KNIFE

RULER

STAPLER

**1.** Trace the pattern on page 27 onto a piece of dark construction paper and cut it out. If your face is longer than the pattern, alter the length of your tracing before you copy it onto the paper.

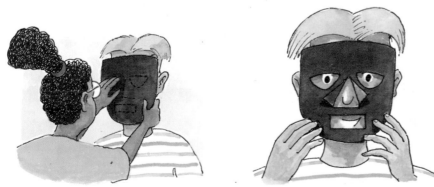

**2.** Hold the cut-out mask against your face and ask a friend to check that the eyeholes and mouth holes are in the right place before you cut them out. Check the position of the nose hole too, then cut along the dotted lines and open out the flaps.

**3.** Cut out two pieces of cream-colored paper, big enough to cover the mask's eyeholes. Draw a small circle in the middle of each piece. Cut out both circles and glue the eyepieces to the back of the eyeholes on the mask.

GLUE

GLUE

**4.** Cut out a strip of dark paper, slightly longer than the mask's mouth. Glue some paper teeth onto this strip, and bend it twice at each end as shown.

**5.** Snip away the corners of the strip and glue it to the back of the mask's mouth, as shown.

**6.** Fold a piece of dark-colored paper in half and draw a nose on it. Make sure that the straight edge of the nose is along the fold and that the curved edge is longer than the flaps on the mask.

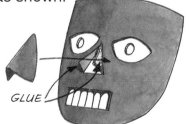

GLUE

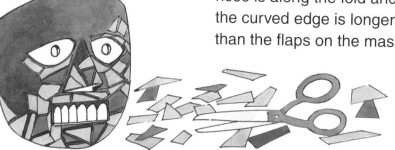

**7.** Cut around the nose, open it out, and glue it to the flaps.

**8.** Cut the adhesive-backed paper into small shapes. Stick the shapes, one by one, onto the mask until it is completely covered.

**9.** To strengthen the forehead, glue a band of paper to the back of the mask, just above the eyeholes. Before you staple the strip of elastic to this band, check that the elastic is long enough to reach from one side of your head, around the back to the other side. If you pull the mask around your face too tightly, the paper shapes may peel off.

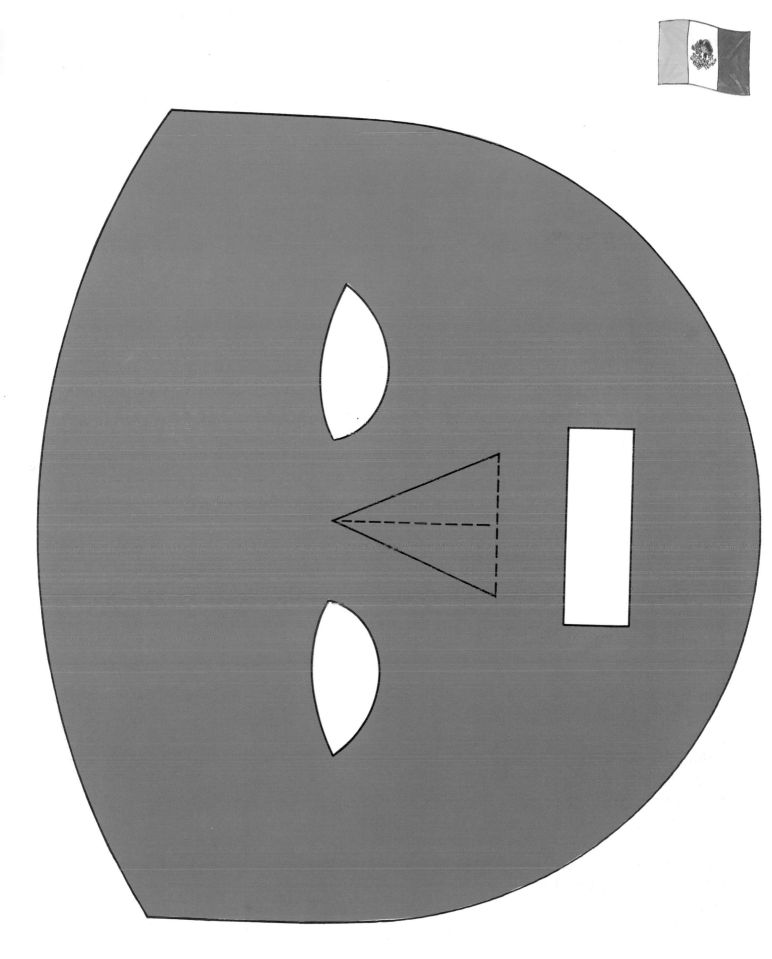

# Mexican History 2

## THE SPANISH ARRIVE

The Spanish discovered Mexico, and the wealth of the Aztecs, in 1517. In 1519, Hernando Cortés arrived in Mexico. The Aztec emperor, Montezuma, sent gifts for Cortés, believing him to be the god, Quetzalcoatl. In return, he was taken hostage. It was not long before the Spanish, with the help of their own horses and cannon, and the Aztecs' Indian enemies, had destroyed this great empire.

## UNDER SPANISH RULE

King Charles I of Spain allowed the Indians to keep their own languages and some of their own form of government. But he insisted that they pay a tax, called a tribute, and convert to the Roman Catholic religion. Many of the Spanish conquistadors behaved cruelly, killing any Indians who resisted them.

## THE FIGHT FOR INDEPENDENCE

On September 15, 1810, a priest named Miguel Hidalgo y Costilla called upon all Mexicans to rebel against Spanish rule and fight for control of their own country. The speech he made that night is the one repeated by the Mexican president every year on Independence Day. He won some support but was soon captured and killed by Spanish troops. In 1820, however, another group of rebels had more success. Mexico finally gained its independence from Spain in 1821.

D. MIGUEL HIDALGO,
Cura del pueblo de Dolores en la provincia de Guanajuato.

## THE MEXICAN REVOLUTION

In 1910, a wealthy landowner, Francisco Madero, led a campaign to overthrow the unpopular president, Porfirio Díaz. Bands of revolutionaries fought against government troops all over Mexico. In 1911, Díaz was forced to resign, to stop any further bloodshed. Madero became president but was assassinated in 1913.

## MEXICAN EARTHQUAKE

In September 1985, Mexico City was hit by a terrible earthquake. More than 8,000 people died and thousands more were left homeless. Among the hundreds of buildings destroyed was the city's maternity hospital. Against the odds, about 50 babies survived being buried under the dust and rubble.

### TIME BAND

| | |
|---|---|
| c. 2000 B.C. | The first villages develop in Mexico |
| 1200–400 B.C. | The Olmec civilization |
| 500 B.C.–A.D.1450 | The Maya civilization |
| A.D. 900–1200 | The Toltec civilization |
| 1300–1521 | The Aztec civilization |
| 1350s | The Aztecs build their capital city, Tenochtitlán |
| 1519 | Hernando Cortés arrives in Mexico |
| 1521 | The last Aztec emperor surrenders |
| 1810–1821 | The struggle for independence |
| 1821 | Mexico gains its independence |
| 1846–1848 | The Mexican War – America wins large areas of Mexican land |
| 1910 | The Mexican Revolution |
| 1985 | Earthquakes hit Mexico City |

**Say it in Spanish**
*historia* – history
*emperador* – emperor
*rey* – king
*calendario* – calendar
*dios* – god
*temple* – temple
*iglesia* – church
*caballo* – horse
*soldado* – soldier

# Picture Pairs

Play Picture Pairs and see how many of the Spanish words in this book you actually remember! The instructions given here are for two to four players, but as your Spanish vocabulary increases, you might like to make more cards and include more players.

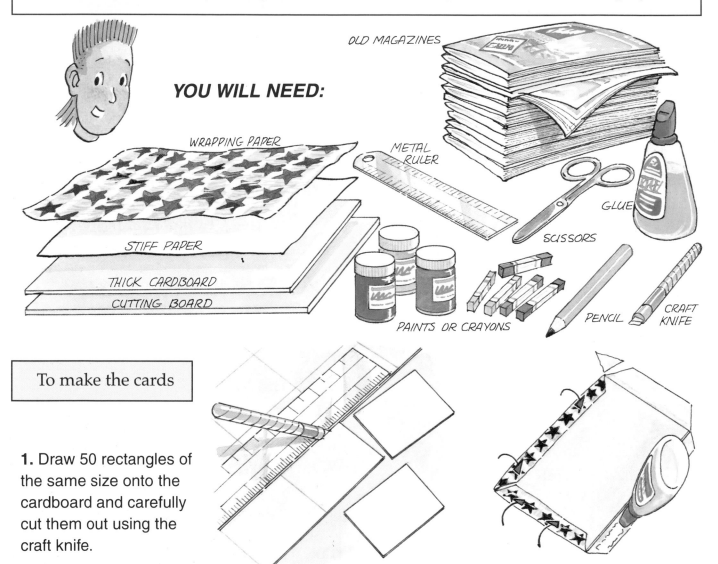

YOU WILL NEED:

OLD MAGAZINES

WRAPPING PAPER

METAL RULER

GLUE

SCISSORS

STIFF PAPER

THICK CARDBOARD

CUTTING BOARD

PAINTS OR CRAYONS

PENCIL

CRAFT KNIFE

## To make the cards

**1.** Draw 50 rectangles of the same size onto the cardboard and carefully cut them out using the craft knife.

**2.** Draw another 50 rectangles onto the wrapping paper and cut them out too. These rectangles should be about three quarters of an inch (2 cm) longer and wider than the cardboard ones.

**3.** Cut the corners of the paper rectangles as shown and glue them onto your cards.

**4.** Draw 25 rectangles, slightly smaller than your cards, onto the stiff paper and cut them out.

**5.** Choose 25 Spanish words from this book and write them down with their English translations. (Keep this list beside you when you play the game.)

**6.** Look through the magazines and cut out any photographs which illustrate the words you have chosen. If you can't find suitable pictures, cut out some more rectangles from stiff paper and paint pictures of your words on them.

El Pan

La Montaña

El Regalo

El Baile

La Culebra

**7.** Stick each photograph or picture onto the front of one of your cards. Glue the stiff paper rectangles onto the rest of the pack and write a Spanish word from your list on each one.

**To play the game**
The object of Picture Pairs is to collect pairs of cards made up of words and their matching picture.

Each player starts the game with seven cards. The rest of the pack is placed face down on the table. If you have any pairs, put them on the table in front of you.

Then ask one of the other players if he/she has a card that you need to make a pair. If that player has the card requested, he/she must hand it over and you win the pair and have another turn. If he/she does not have the card, you take a card from the pack in the middle and the turn passes to the next person.

All word cards must be translated into English. If you cannot remember the translation of the word, look it up and miss your next go.

The player who pairs all his cards first is the winner.

# Index

Additional Photographs:
AA Photo Library P. 17; A.G. Formenti P. 21; All Sport Photographic Ltd. P. 18; Bridgeman P. 14; J. Allan Cash Ltd.; Bruce Coleman P. 24; P. 14; Gamma P. 9; Robert Harding P. 9, 12, 14, 24, 29; Hutchison P. 4, 7, 12, 13, 22; Mexicolore P. 22, 29; South American Pictures P. 19, 20; Frank Spooner P. 19, 20; Werner Forman Archive P. 23, 25; Zefa P. 6, 7, 8, 15, 20 Cover.